AF596734

Table of contents

Hindrances to destiny

bad parenting and family cause is a destiny killer

Dop Moses

Chapter 1

The truth about destiny (predetermination)

I have this inquiry as a primary concern with me unfit to sort out the truth. I frequently hear individuals say your predetermination is in your grasp. Likewise, I heard somebody say his predetermination is in the possession of God. The inquiry is .

YOUR Fate IS IN YOUR Grasp OR IN THE Possession OF GOD?

Are you and you becoming the same thing since you arranged yourself or because that is how God arranged it since you were conceived?
Pls I really want sensible responses
Perhaps the most widely recognized restricting element that I see in many individuals' lives is their convictions about their fate. For such countless individuals, this word has been stacked with supernatural importance and consequently is just grasped by the profound world _class. Subsequently, many simply pass on their way of living to a higher power and live every day trusting that something will happen that will make them carry on with a superior life.

The entertaining thing here is that individuals will remark on everything their Ministers and Prophets said to them with next to no private examination. What's more, the strict ones will consider this to be a valuable chance to communicate or feature their proclaiming abilities since they don't have a platform yet. By and by I think a people's predetermination is a Divine being given way that everybody should follow and it works following your motivation as if God has foreordained you to be a donor, you should follow the correct way to your fate or follow some unacceptable way. For that reason we were given personalities to think, hands and legs to help. You must find your actual mission and when you find you begin pursuing it. Something else I found is the truth of mysticism. It is genuine and to that end, predeterminations could be controlled (deferred) yet can never be traded. A lunatic today that was bound to be a lord is as yet distraught the became can't help himself, regardless of whether he has found, he wants to stroll toward it.

Another is the standard of timing. It assumes an extremely extraordinary part in this subject of predetermination since everything adjusts to its standards. At a specific time, "this should be" and genuinely, you can't transform it however you can control it through mysticism. The
Reality with regards to Predetermination

In any case, is that reality about predetermination?A magical power that shapes our lives unwittingly and conveys us down a way fitting its personal preference? Or on the other , d is it something significantly more basic that is controlling our way of living?

Peruse on to find reality with regard to your fate.

WHAT'S CONTROLLING YOUR Predetermination?
Predetermination is one of those words that implies a wide range of things to various individuals. For some purposes, it implies the power of destiny that controls the universe and impacts our lives. For other people, it implies a definitive arrangement of God that our lives have been pre arranged to perform. What's more, for some, it has practically no importance since they don't carry on with their lives in yielding to a higher power.

Fate Statement - William Jennings BryanDestiny comes from a similar root word in Latin that gives us "objective." Basically, predetermination is one more approach to saying where your way is taking you. Furthermore, what coordinates our ways throughout everyday life? God? Destiny? Possibility? Or on the other hand is it something different?

As a matter of fact we as a whole know the awkward truth that stands up to each individual on this planet is that our choices control our fate. Yet, for some reasons, we would rather not just own it.

Clearly, you can perceive how this reality that our choices decide our predetermination comes into gigantic struggle with the conviction that so many of us hold dear that God or the Universe is arranging the conditions of our lives. Be that as it may, eventually, who's the party in question for where you're going? Is it God who put you this way or is it you?

WHO'S Liable FOR WHERE YOU'RE GOING?
Consider it. When did you last hear somebody discussing their conditions express something as, "I don't have the foggiest idea how this occurred!" Constantly, correct? Furthermore, it's generally when things are going inadequately and they've pursued a few choices that conveyed serious outcomes into their lives.

At the point when we accept that some different option from ourselves is controlling our fate then we give ourselves the reason to continue to pursue similar choices and expect various outcomes. What's more, that, as broadly characterized by Albert Einstein, is madness.

Predetermination Choice Statement - Tony RobbinsFor model, I got around 50% of an episode of High schooler Mother 3 while flipping through the diverts in my lodging recently. Presently, it doesn't take a technical genius to sort out how these young fellows and ladies wound up in this way. They pursued a ton of small choices that hinted right when they chose to have unprotected sex with each other and afterward wound up burdened with the obligation of being a parent.

However, did they stop the frenzy of their unfortunate dynamic after they had infants? Obviously not! Since who needs to assume a sense of ownership with their choices when they can put them on some other person or thing? Correct?

Right. Furthermore, that is the human condition, companions. Left uncontrolled, we'll fault pretty much anything around us as opposed to getting a sense of ownership with our prospects. Tragically, a significant number of us just understand the reality that it was our choices that decided our fate unreasonably late to change the outcomes of our activities.

All in all, where is your way taking you? Might it be said that you are content with where your life is going or is it time for a course remedy? Truly, it depends on you.

In some cases, God can give us dreams that appear to be totally unimaginable and practically unfathomable.

A couple of individuals hop in, and they trail closely behind those fantasies no matter what the dangers, confiding in God in the unexplored world. Many individuals, however, feel uncertain in view of things that are keeping them away from following God with practically no preventions.

We really want to have a change in outlook where we perceive that we have a major, strong Dad who loves and supports us and is complicatedly engaged with our lives.

Various things will attempt to keep us away from perceiving our sonship and satisfying our fate, however the following are not many that I've found in my life and others'.

1. Unimportance

This is quite possibly the most widely recognized thing that I see preventing individuals from being who they genuinely are and venturing out in strength and certainty.

Unimportance is an enemy of fate, confidence, and connections. According to this negative mental self portrait, 'I'm not sufficient' or 'I don't have the stuff'.

Somebody who battles with irrelevance generally believes that they're second-best or somebody's subsequent option to finish a work, and they battle with uncertainty in themselves and in God.

Instructions to Say 'NO!' to Irrelevance

Quite possibly the most ideal way I've found to battle unimportance is to begin with little strides by doing things that challenge you to step up to the plate.

The best way to see that you can do what God has requested that you do is to simply do them. Truly we don't have the innate capacity to do what God has asked us to, however assuming that He has called us to follow through with something, He will enable us to make it happen. Encircle yourself with individuals who will advocate and support you in the fantasies that God has given you.

Something else to comprehend is that it's OK to request help. A way that irrelevance can pop up is to show itself as self-importance.

At the point when we In all actuality do take something on, we need to demonstrate that we can do it without anyone's help with no assistance since 'we have the stuff'. In this back to front, topsy turvy Realm we live in, once in a while we can understand our most prominent assets when we make a stride back in modesty. Besides, filling in as a group is in every case better compared to doing it single-handedly.

'In any case, God has picked the silly things of the world to humiliate the astute, and God has picked the powerless things of the world to embarrass the things which are strong; and the base things of the world and the things which are detested God has picked, and the things which are not, to bring to nothing the things that are.'
(1 Corinthians 1:27-28)

2. Dread

Dread is demonstrated to find actual success at leaving us speechless concerning our future.

On the off chance that we allow dread to administer in one region, it can deaden us in different regions, as well. Dread isn't our legacy: love, harmony, and delight are. According to dread, 'That is excessively frightening', 'I could get injured', 'It's excessively perilous/new/and so forth', or 'I'm as well (abnormal/uproarious/timid/unique/and so on)'. Dread and intelligence are totally different things.

Assuming you're a Christian going to a Muslim country, a few insight and heading from God is expected to get by, yet in light of the fact that it's hazardous, that doesn't imply that it's unthinkable or ought not be finished.

Dread shows itself in a wide range of ways. I, for one, battle with dread in the space of dread of dismissal and I continually need to say, 'No. I'm adored, I'm acknowledged, and it's alright on the off chance that I'm unique.' Particularly when I begin to feel misconstrued or judged wrongly.

Apprehension about the obscure is another that is pervasive. Individuals don't have the foggiest idea or don't have any idea so they simply disregard it or they reject it totally.

Instructions to Say 'NO!' to Dread

Dread is a troublesome one to battle, yet this is where 'reestablishing of the brain' (Romans 12:2) and 'kidnapping of your viewpoints' (2 Corinthians 10:4-6) is so significant.

Like I referenced previously, I battle with dread of dismissal, yet it's getting more straightforward. I need to prepare my psyche to think uniquely in contrast to what I did previously. Before God drew this issue out into the open, I would allow my considerations to run with horrendous contemplations like, 'I won't ever fit in' or 'I'm simply excessively unique to them.' I would allow these considerations to take over until the apprehension was deplorable and I would either separate myself to stay away from dismissal or I would be the one to dismiss first.

Presently when these contemplations attempt to assume control over me, I'm ready to perceive that it's not reality and to close the idea down before it's ready to begin unleashing destruction on my heart. I'll then, at that point, think the inverse and discuss reality to me. This sounds unimportant, yet beautiful. Soon my capacity to think reality rather than falsehood becomes more straightforward and the unfortunate considerations no longer hold any longer.

Helping ourselves to remember the reality of what God says regarding us is critical to developing our mental fortitude, strength, and trust notwithstanding unnerving circumstances. These are 2 sections that stick out to me with respect to fear:

'For God has not provided us with a feeling of dread, but rather of force and of adoration and of a sound psyche.'
(2 Timothy 1:7)

"For I know the contemplations that I think toward you, says the Ruler, considerations of harmony and not of malevolence, to give you a future and an expectation.'
(Jeremiah 29:11)

3. Funds
This is one that truly strikes a chord for me. Commonly, as a teacher, the issue of funds is something that you are continually pondering.

This can be one of the greatest hang-ups with pursuing your predetermination, particularly assuming that it includes travel as well as charitable effort. Living as a worker abroad is a remarkable confidence venture as, more often than not, you can't work (since it's unlawful), so you rely upon loved ones who support you monetarily to in a real sense assist you with continuing to live.

I hear individuals say, 'Gracious, I want to go to (embed country name here), however it's excessively costly' or 'I couldn't want anything more than to go on this mission trip, yet I need more cash.'

By and large, I make about $25/day as a teacher, however it vacillates enormously. Clearly, this is WAY under the lowest pay permitted by law. Some way or another, I went to EIGHT nations last year. The math has neither rhyme nor reason. I likewise pay lease, telephone bill, and staff expenses, I purchase my own food, and I support different preachers. Some way or another, I have never gone hungry or been not able to pay my lease.

It is simply because of God that I am ready to do what I do, and I do it since I realize He needs me to. He is unwavering! You need more cash? Sure you don't, however God does! He claims everything!

Step by step instructions to Say 'NO!' to Funds Keeping You Down

I think this is one reason why Jesus says you can't serve God and mammon, which additionally implies abundance (Matthew 6:24). At the point when we put our cash or material abundance before God's course, we're making it a symbol.

God is completely in charge of our funds, alongside all the other things. We won't bring our cash with us into time everlasting, however the fortunes that will be put away in paradise for us when we follow Jesus to unimaginable lengths will be worth undeniably more eventually.

Try not to let the paper that the world has placed esteem in be worth more than the future that GOD has composed for you. Step out. Believe Him.

'Thusly sit back and relax, expressing out loud, 'Whatever will we eat?' or 'What will we drink?' or 'What will we wear?' For after everything the Gentiles look for. For your radiant Dad realizes that you want everything. In any case, look into the realm of God and His uprightness, and everything will be added to you.'
(Matt. 6:31-33)

4. Vagrant Attitude and Natural Viewpoint
These two are somewhat comprehensive issues that truly keep us away from our predetermination.

In this fallen, severe world, it tends to be not difficult to feel alone and like everything is tremendously hard. At the point when we check out, it is so natural to fall into a frenzy and vulnerability about our future. It can appear as though things are going to pieces on various levels.

We as a whole go through these times, yet certain individuals stroll in these mindsets frequently. At the point when we battle with these two things, or even one of them, we can tend to have a level view, rather than an upward one. We can take a gander at this world and our lives with a pessimist mentality, where we need to battle for all that or battle for no good reason.

Vagrants need to fight, handle, and search for everything. They live in a 'natural selection' world and once in a while, even as devotees of Jesus, we carry on that way, as well, despite the fact that we have all that we really want accessible to us constantly.

The 'Vagrant Attitude' is where we don't completely get a handle on our reception (Ephesians 1:5) in Jesus Christ. The Vagrant Mindset keeps us away from our fate since we do everything from a position of endeavoring.

With a Natural Point of view, it can feel like we're dependent upon the limits of this world concerning the things that we can do with our lives. It's not difficult to see the clatter for to an ever increasing extent and MORE achievement and to need to ascend that stepping stool, too, particularly in North American culture.

We as a whole realize that the quest for bliss is brief and in the long run purposeless.

Step by step instructions to Say 'NO!' to a Vagrant Attitude and a Natural Viewpoint
The way to express no to a Vagrant Mindset and a Natural Point of view is to peruse the Expression of God. It appears to be a straightforward response, however God loves to discuss who He's made us to be in the Good book.

This is another of those things, similar to fear, where it boils down to a reestablishing of our psyches which just accompanies investing energy with the Dad and perusing and paying attention to what He needs to say regarding us (which is in every case great).

If you at any point hope to know how God so unpredictably sees you, read Hymn 139 once more. Peruse it through the eyes of a His Dad kid without measure, yet additionally through the eyes of the Ruler of the universe who has all power, control, domain, and you in His grasp… consistently.

Since we are taken on in Jesus' family, Ephesians 2:6 says that we are situated with Him in brilliant spots. We ought to have the point of view of paradise, not the viewpoint of earth as a result of our situation at the right hand of the Dad.

All in all, we as a whole have things that we battle with, and a few things might appear to be more terrible than others, yet actually we really want to recollect that we serve a steadfast God who needs to make things right more than we do.

He is the solution to us satisfying our fates.

However long we continue to seek after Him, we're doing great.

Try not to let your deficiencies (we as a whole got them) keep you away from your fate

Chapter 2

Wrong accomplice destroy destiny (wrong partner)

We as a whole have a fate, a task to be satisfied, a specific greatness relegated for your elevation yet a few things can influence it, a piece of which is relationship.

The individual you decide to use the remainder of your existence with can make or blemish your fate, trust me. We will consider a few sorts of connections that can influence your predetermination.

1. Relationship with an unbeliever

The Good book cautions against being inconsistent burdened in 2 Cor. 6:14. That refrain just signifies, "Don't become accomplices with the individuals who reject God." When you admit Christ and acknowledge Him, you move from murkiness into light, you become a city that is set on the slope. Thus, going into a long-lasting seal with somebody still in dimness will just cause more damage than great.

2. Relationship without God

Indeed, you're the two devotees however did you include God all along? A decent devotee to your eye may not be the great decision God has for yourself and may modify your predetermination.

3. Sexual Relationship

'Marriage is good and the bed immaculate' (Heb. 13:4a) A relationship including sex is clearly not getting approval from God sex actually stays a useful asset in the hand of Satan to frustrate such countless predeterminations.

4. Deliberate relationship

It appears to be hanging tight for the ideal individual will be always, trust conceded is presently making the heart feeble and you go for your own decision. This is actually an expensive misstep, ask those that are in this present circumstance, on the off chance that they will come clean with you, they will let you know its damnation. Allow God to start to lead the pack so your decision will not obliterate you.

5. Surged Relationship.

Hurrying into a relationship to stay away from 'depression' or 'singlehood' or in light of the fact that everybody around you is by all accounts in one is something else that influences a few fates. Try not to permit anyone to cause you to do what you are not intellectually, inwardly, monetarily and profoundly ready for. Many promising connections are annihilated for absence of astute premonition, lost philosophy about male/female sexuality, and maltreatment of human closeness. Never hurry into a relationship or you will rush out yet recollect you can't be the equivalent again going out!

6. Inconspicuous Relationship

Indeed, they exist. These are a greater amount of profound subjugations, soul spouse/wives, masturbation, erotic entertainment, sex dreams and the preferences are associations that can obliterate your wonderful fate.

This isn't simply an article, it is a mindfulness for petition, to find and recuperate anything that you have lost. You will cry and say Father, convey me, eliminate me from each relationship known or obscure that can annihilate my predetermination, set me free and assist me with taking cues from you generally.

This is a significant business, you really want to ask that request in order to partake in your predetermination. Enough of demons playing with your life, the time has come to reclaim what Satan has taken from you.
Terrible climate
What climate means for our fate

A few men appear to draw in progress, influence, riches and fulfillment with very little cognizant exertion, you will find such individuals being viewed as fortunate, others are supposed to be leaned toward by destiny and the require their predeterminations. The unpleasant truth is that their environmental elements wouldn't be of much appreciation as certain rivals to them will characterize and affirm the force of devils and shamefulness in them making a ton of dread, disdain and dismissal around their area. Such individuals are so fortunate for a reality in that you will count their front dads and, surprisingly, their relatives to follow the suit making life a simple, fascinating and direct way.

Others vanquish existence with extraordinary trouble, difficulties and penances. Individuals in this class will be battling since birth to shape their future and have a go at making their lives of their relatives endlessly better than that of their predecessors. They focus on things that are impossible for them, they do any sorts of positions vigorously, basically to cook for their necessities including educational expenses and when they graduate, they land in the area to look for occupations confronting such countless difficulties. The battle closes not yet, when they land positions, they over-work with incredible go for the gold, and venture. In any case, toward the day's end, they become pleased to make it as it were.

Tragically, others will do everything of their strength yet at the same time bomb out and out, not that they have actual difficulties or mental stupidity but since of

inescapable conditions. This gathering will really hit the books, buckle down, save, stay safe yet their karma is generally processed by such countless adversities that they know not how to dodge from. They would be named unfortunate, reviled and would try to be named untouchables. It gets incredibly difficult for them to make
closes meet.

In my decision I will attempt to portray the reason for this. What simplifies life for some, hard for other people and, surprisingly, incredibly hard for one more gathering. Take this visit in light of me and have this image. A youngster who is brought into the world in the states will study, get utilized and bring in bunches of cash (a fair arrangement I think). In like manner, a youngster would be brought into the world in a rich family and need not much training to acquire his fortune. Flipping the image to the opposite side, one more kid would be brought into the world in an unfortunate family and in an unfortunate nation, really hit the books entirely hard just to find a loser line of work whence confronting every one of the obligations up from family the whole way to local area. This will just imply that our fates and fortunes rotate around our encompassing climate.

Chapter 3

Fear; the destiny killer

Can not to Allow fearTo control Your destiny
Do you accept that fear has become one of the significant elements which has begun affecting terrifically significant choices of your life and consequently restricting your development prospects and demolishing bliss throughout everyday life? If so, the time has finally come for us to begin recognizing and pursuing conquering this deficiency in our character.

Dread makes advances in our day to day existence from youth days

Have you at any point pondered that as a kid our greatest trepidation is of losing our folks? We petition God for the long existence of our folks. One reason for this dread is obviously our affection towards our folks. What's more, another explanation might be our weakness. We realize that we are little and can't deal with ourselves. We want guardians to deal with our fooding, clothing, haven, instruction or more all necessity for adoration and love.

Society assumes a significant part in forming our reactions to fear

Our characters are formed by our folks, however our educators, companions, colleagues, family members, seniors and virtual entertainment likewise have a profound impact in our lives. Individuals are great duplicate felines. However they possess brainpower of their own, yet not many of them really dedicate time and psyche to make an assessment on what is correct and what's going on. The majority of the time, we acknowledge things how they are around us without scrutinizing its holiness.

We see that when individuals bomb in their endeavors, all around society ridicules them, deters them from giving it another attempt, and have a mediocrity feeling towards individuals who flop in their endeavors. Then again, effective individuals are dealt with like genuine geniuses. Society just recollects their victories failing to remember the steady disappointments they needed to defeat prior to becoming effective.

Simultaneously, the second fruitful individuals begin coming up short, society quickly begins censuring these individuals too. So the pattern is to place you large and in charge till the time you are succeeding and the second you begin fizzling, lose you from the top.

This is more apparent if there should be an occurrence of lawmakers, sports people and film stars. Never of time is there an acknowledgment regarding how much exertion and difficult work that has happened for a really long time to make an individual truly prevail throughout everyday life. Might you at any point remove the credit of the long lasting battling soul of an individual in light of disappointments in life for a brief timeframe?

How dread beginnings controlling our dynamic interaction

As we become older, a feeling of dread toward disappointment and the response of individuals who matter for us begins influencing our dynamic cycle incredibly. Rather than investing amounts of energy and extending ourselves to accomplish higher development and focuses throughout everyday life, we begin cutting back our objectives and assumptions from life so we don't bomb throughout everyday life.

The principal thing we do is dump our imagination, enthusiasm and our area of interest throughout everyday life. Rather we choose a course in school that will give a task with consistent pay throughout everyday life. We essentially disdain the sensation of frailty that comes from monetary vulnerability. So to defeat our apprehension about instability, we pick to make a protected vocation as a representative of an enormous partnership as opposed to selecting being independently employed as an expert. As an independently employed Proficient, we would have worked for ourselves sustaining our ability and carrying on with a free proficient existence liberated from dread of losing our employment.

"To get away from dread, you need to go through it, not around" by Richie Norton

However, to fulfill momentary feelings of trepidation, we thought twice about our drawn out development. Also, in the long haul, we will constantly stay in the hold of dread of losing our employment since we never figured out how to autonomously bring in cash.

On the off chance that we could beat the craving for a safe life, we might have settled on a vocation as a business visionary or an entrepreneur. As business visionaries, we have the choice of utilizing the abilities and skills of other people who could be representatives; independently employed experts, other entrepreneurs or financial backers.

Fruitful organizations are controlled by individuals who exhibit incredible initiative characteristics and who foster such frameworks and cycles that experts maintain their organizations. This helps money managers invest more energy in thinking and extending their organizations with the assistance of their groups. At last they can get their life as well as have the fulfillment of giving work to such countless individuals.

Dread creates its shaded area in varying backgrounds

Dread can influence your character in numerous ways. Assuming you are a thoughtful person, apprehension about dismissal prevents you from systems administration and making new companions. It prevents you from looking for help from others when you are out of luck. This way you lose amazing open doors in any event, when somebody might have helped you out.

"Dread is a propensity, self indulgence, rout, uneasiness, depression, sadness and renunciation is as well. You can wipe out this large number of negative propensities with two basic purposes, "I can! also, I will!"." By Obscure

We as a whole need to have discussions at various places of time. It may very well be while purchasing a property, looking for pay rates or better profiles in interviews, fixing relationships for kids, buying exorbitant things and so on. The individuals who dread that others might chuckle at their recommendations will eventually get directed by other individual's agreements.

Apprehension about society and depression in life are the fundamental purposes behind a ton of ladies not to dissent and eventually continue with their hopeless wedded lives.

On account of dread of forlornness throughout everyday life, a lot of old individuals keep living with their youngsters even subsequent to enduring embarrassment because of kids.

Feeling of dread toward frustrating others or getting yourself disheartened prevents you from facing challenges throughout everyday life and unloading those choices which you would somehow have taken as a consistent and normal individual.

Number of disappointments will constantly be more than the achievements throughout everyday life

The conviction that thinking twice about our qualities, trying not to have difficulties or lower down our objectives and assumptions from life will give us a protected, secure and it isn't right to satisfy life.

Life will continue to toss difficulties at us. We can't stay away from that. We really want to overwhelm the Evil presence of Dread of Disappointment that has assumed command over our Brain. We really want to toss this Devil crazy.

What we fizzle to comprehend is that the number of quantity of accomplishments throughout everyday life. There will be such countless endeavors thus numerous disappointments before we at last succeed. This is the manner by which life works. Yet, assuming we begin accepting that prior disappointments are the

Last objections throughout everyday life, then, at that point, we will lose the Self discipline to carry on the clash of difficulties in life, eventually missing out throughout everyday life. Achievement will constantly stay the last objective and Disappointments are simply stopping places in the excursion of life.

Chapter 4

Pardon kill destiny

On the off chance that you incredibly need something, you track down a way.
In the event that you don't feel deserving of it, you come up with a rationalization.

Smooth talking enormously influences your certainty and your confidence.

Smooth talking is self destructive behavior. A negative conduct disrupts your capacities, execution and inspiration. An interruption and evasion conduct keeps you from getting what you ridiculously care about. It comes from a more profound, subliminal longing to safeguard yourself (your Inner self) against uneasiness and disgrace. The more restless or embarrassed you're probably going to feel, the more certain you are to construct hindrances that slow down your capacity to accomplish what you extremely care about.

When a collaborator inquires: "How about you go for that advancement?"
Excuse: "They won't give it to me in any case, for what reason would it be advisable for me to have trouble."

When a companion inquires: "How about you emerge to this occasion with my companions?"
Excuse: "I won't know anybody, and I have activities at home."

At the point when you ponder internally: "I truly need to transform myself and be more joyful."
Pardons: "It's excessively hard." or "I'll get it done later." or "I can sort it out all alone."

Rationalizing to others is a certain something, yet it is absolutely disastrous to rationalize to yourself. Individuals do it so frequently that it turns into a constant reaction. Be that as it may, have you at any point contemplated the monstrous adverse consequences it has on you? At the point when you rationalize yourself, you are telling yourself that you don't have the determination, confidence or self-esteem, AND you're letting your nervousness and fears direct your life. You're likewise saying that you decide to surrender and not take the necessary steps to figure out how to get it going for yourself - doing so makes it incomprehensible for you to have outright certainty.

Obviously, there is a contrast between rationalizing and giving clarifications. On the off chance that you are giving a clarification, you are taking on obligation and confronting the outcomes. Also, with a clarification and lucidity you can dissect, and by breaking down you can comprehend and learn.

Assuming that you are coming up with a rationalization, you are not tolerating liability and not confronting the outcomes. You are searching for a simple "way out".

The truth of the matter is that on the off chance that you incredibly need something, you can get it going assuming you keep at it sufficiently long. Regardless of your conditions. You essentially need to stop rationalizing and begin creating open doors.

On the other side, in the event that you genuinely don't extremely believe you should follow through with something, then feel free to possess it, and just own it to yourself as well as other people - and don't provide it with anything else of your valuable energy or consideration.

Rather than investing your energy in "I can't do _______ on the grounds that... ", change everything you say to yourself.
A couple of far additional enabling inquiries to pose to yourself are:

"At any rate, how might I figure out how to do ________?"
"What might I at any point change?"
"Who could help me?"
"What might I at any point do any other way?"

"What might I at any point surrender that truly isn't as essential to me over the long haul?"

Pardons are a method for legitimizing not seeking after what you truly need throughout everyday life. Yet, you're never going to get everything you truly need until you quit saying to yourself why you can't and begin making a day to day existence that demonstrates that you can.

Have you known about this astounding man? Scratch Vujicic. He was brought into the world without arms and legs. After a youth of harassing and contemplations of self destruction, he is presently quite possibly the best persuasive orator on the planet! He's so extraordinary, I have Such a lot of regard for him!!!

He says:
"You might still have arms and legs except if you know 3 things…
#1) Who are you, and what your worth is.
#2) What is your motivation here throughout everyday life?
#3) What your fate is.
On the off chance that you don't have a clue about the solutions to ANY of those 3 inquiries, you are more crippled than I."

Chapter 5

Awful nurturing can affect destiny in negative way (bad parenting)

Awful nurturing can be characterized as deficient help from guardians for their kids in a profound, mental, scholarly or actual way.

Terrible youngster raising can cause serious unfriendly impacts, including mental as well as actual harm for the individual kids.

Reasons for Terrible Nurturing
Drug use
Undesirable youngster
Vanity
Mental issues
Actual medical problems
Neediness
Joblessness
Straining
Profession desires
Separate
Dissatisfaction
Absence of schooling
Drug use
Awful nurturing

In the event that your folks are dependent on legitimate medications like liquor or unlawful medications, they may presently not have the option to deal with you in an adequate way since drug fiends frequently care more about how they can guarantee their substance supply than about dealing with their kids.

Thus, in the event that you experience childhood in a family where your folks consume drugs, you might experience the ill effects of serious disregard.

Undesirable kid

A few guardians are very glad to get kids. In any case, a few guardians are not ready for itself as well as their youngsters are fairly a sort of mishap.

These supposed undesirable kids will frequently not be dealt with that well since guardians haven't wanted to get them and probably won't deal with these youngsters.

Additionally, these guardians may likewise not have the option to bring their kids up in a legitimate way since they basically haven't arranged themselves and don't have the foggiest idea what's significant.

Pride

A few guardians are likewise very self important and care substantially more about themselves and their advancement in life than about the psychological and actual wellbeing of their kids.

Assuming that you experience childhood in such a family, odds are you might experience the ill effects of extreme disregard and other mental issues since you probably won't feel significant by any means.

This issue turns out to be far and away more terrible assuming pride transforms into serious degrees of self-centered conduct of guardians.

Mental issues

Guardians with psychological wellness issues may likewise not have the option to deal with their youngsters in a legitimate way.

For example, assuming your folks experience the ill effects of mental issues like fantasies or schizophrenia, odds are they can barely deal with their own life and you as a kid should deal with yourself from a very early age on.

Mental issues of guardians may likewise transform into actual medical problems for kids in the event that these psychological issues make guardians misuse their youngsters.

Actual medical problems

Guardians may likewise not have the option to help their youngsters in an adequate way because of actual handicaps.

For example, in the event that your folks depend on a wheelchair to move around, they can not go out to shop or to cook for you as a kid.

They may likewise not have the option to carry you to school and their handicap might forestall them to achieve a few different errands in their day to day routine.

In this way, your folks will most likely be unable to deal with you in a legitimate way.

You as a kid might try and need to help them all things being equal.

Neediness

One more justification for awful nurturing might be destitution.

Assuming that you experience childhood in a family where neediness is a major issue, odds are your folks will be unable to guarantee you with legitimate schooling and different things that could work on your opportunities for your future life.

Neediness may likewise prompt serious degrees of sadness and dissatisfaction for your folks, which might expand the possibilities of youngster misuse or other antagonistic ramifications for their kids.

Joblessness

Joblessness might be one more element with regards to awful nurturing.

On the off chance that your folks are jobless, your family might experience the ill effects of huge degrees of neediness, which might keep you from getting legitimate schooling, particularly assuming that you live in an unfortunate non-industrial nation.

In addition, joblessness may likewise prompt psychological well-being issues for your folks, which might additionally build the gamble of unfortunate kid raising.

Moreover, likewise your possibilities of becoming jobless once you grow up increments, since kids take on numerous qualities of their folks and may act along these lines once they transform into adults.

Straining

Guardians may likewise be very wrecked by the sheer measure of work youngsters generally request.

Subsequently, a few guardians will most likely be unable to manage this multitude of issues and may likewise not set forth this energy.

This might prompt disregard and a few different issues for the separate kids.

Profession desires

In many organizations, despite the fact that organizations guarantee to help the confidential existence of representatives, joining a family with an aggressive career is still very hard.

Subsequently, in families where the two guardians have a requesting position, kids might experience this because folks will work very extended periods and will be unable to deal with their youngsters in an adequate way.

Separate

A separation is a fairly upsetting thing that can convert into a few issues, including questions in regards to material products yet additionally with respect to who will be capable to deal with the kids.

Assuming this debate gains out of influence, kids may frequently need to grow up with just a single parent and may experience the ill effects of this in a close to home way.

Dissatisfaction

Contingent upon a few circumstances, life can be very intense for certain individuals.

Individuals may frequently feel to be dealt with unjustifiably leaning on an unshakable conviction and may turn out to be very frantic and baffled because of blows of destiny or other serious unfavorable occasions.

This urgency might transform into dissatisfaction, which might convert into youngster maltreatment since certain guardians can't manage what is going on in a genuinely steady way.

Absence of instruction

The way of nurturing additionally fundamentally decides the degree of training of kids.

Assuming guardians are very anxious to furnish their youngsters with instruction materials and furthermore assist them with their schoolwork, odds are good that these kids will actually want to get better grades and to go to better schools and universities contrasted with kids from families where their folks couldn't care less about the training of their kids.

Impacts of Poor Nurturing

Disregard

Mental issues

Issues at school

Low degrees of instruction

Monetary issues

Shakiness

Drug use

Joblessness
Vagrancy
Negative mentality towards life
Disregard
Terrible nurturing can prompt serious disregard for the impacted youngsters.

On the off chance that individuals couldn't care less about their youngsters and don't have any desire to invest adequate energy with them, odds are these kids will feel not significant by any stretch of the imagination.

Besides, in the event that they are not upheld by their folks in regards to significant errands like schoolwork and different things that kids need to deal with, odds are because of disregard, these youngsters might experience the ill effects of serious unexpected issues.

Mental issues
Because of awful nurturing, youngsters may likewise experience the ill effects of serious mental issues.

Since youngsters haven't fostered a steady person yet, they are very defenseless with regards to disregard or different results of terrible nurturing.

Thus, these kids might foster psychological wellness issues like discouragements since they might feel very lost in life because of an absence of help from their folks, particularly in the event that they additionally have unexpected issues in everyday schedule portions of their day to day existence.

Issues at school

Unfortunate childhood may likewise cause difficult issues at school.

For example, in the event that youngsters have issues at school because of harassment, they may not get the essential help and exhortation from their folks to safeguard themselves and may languish over seemingly forever.

In addition, issues at school can likewise incorporate terrible grades.

In the event that youngsters experience the ill effects of poor nurturing, they are bound to get terrible grades and will be unable to go to a school, which might convert them into terrible open positions.

Low degrees of training

Poor nurturing may likewise prompt low degrees of schooling as a general rule, viewing grades as well as in a few different pieces of life.

This could imply that kids may not figure out how to fix things at home or how to continue and take care of specific regular routine issues.

Not realizing those things might prompt difficult issues once these kids transform into adults, since they may frequently feel lost and not ready to tackle their concerns all alone.

Monetary issues

Awful nurturing can likewise prompt monetary issues, for guardians themselves as well as for their youngsters.

For example, assuming you experience childhood in a family where your folks have monetary issues consistently, odds are good that you take on their way of behaving into adulthood and act likewise.

Studies have shown that youngsters are intensely impacted by their folks.

This is likewise valid for monetary points.

Compounding the situation, guardians with monetary issues can likewise not show their kids acceptable behavior monetarily mindful and their youngsters may likewise not learn it in any case.

Untrustworthiness

In the event that youngsters never gain from their folks to be dependable, they might have huge challenges with acting in a solid way once they transform into adults.

In any case, this trickiness might prompt a few issues in their day to day existence, including more regrettable open positions and a few different issues since dependability is a fundamental trademark for prevailing in a few pieces of life.

Drug use

One more issue with awful nurturing is that it expands the gamble for the utilization of specific substances for their kids.

In the event that youngsters feel disregarded and not important, they might spend time with companions rather than their folks for a major part of their whole youth.

Assuming these companions ingest medications, odds are good that because of friend pressure, different kids might follow a similar way.

Thus, this might prompt medication reliance from a moderately early age, which will make it very difficult for those kids to turn out to be perfect.

Joblessness

Because of awful nurturing and the subsequent absence of instruction, youngsters may likewise experience the ill effects of expanded opportunities for terrible open positions and joblessness.

Joblessness may thus prompt a few different issues, including dissatisfaction and chronic drug use.

Vagrancy

In outrageous cases, terrible nurturing may likewise prompt vagrancy for their youngsters in later phases of their life.

Assuming individuals become jobless, they may presently not have the option to pay their lease and end up destitute in the roads.

This is particularly evident in nations where there is no or just lacking federal retirement aid.

When individuals become jobless in those nations, they might slip into vagrancy and the subsequent unfriendly outcomes without any problem.

Negative mentality towards life

As a rule, kids who have been dismissed or manhandled by their folks might foster a very bad mentality towards life because of their terrible cherished recollections.

In any case, a negative disposition towards life prompts a few different issues, including emotional wellness issues.

In this manner, awful nurturing might prompt difficult issues, in adolescence as well as for later stages in the existence of these youngsters.

Answers for Terrible Nurturing
Better help from schools
Organization programs for families
Encourage homes
Mental help
Monetary appropriations
Programs against drug use
Self-reflection
Self-improvement
Upgrades in schooling
Support youngsters in your area
Better help from schools
Kids ought to constantly have the potential chance to get support from schools assuming that they experience the ill effects of terrible nurturing and the subsequent outcomes.

This could imply that schools give after school care where youngsters can get their work done with the assistance of a coach or educator.

Besides, it could likewise mean mental help.

Youngsters ought to have an occasion in school where they can go on the off chance that they get manhandled or experience different issues connected with awful nurturing.

By offering kids these chances, they might get legitimate help and the issues connected with terrible nurturing could be moderated partially.

Organization programs for families

On the off chance that the two guardians have requested a position with long working hours, chiefs in organizations ought to reconsider the organization values toward a path where family and work are more viable.

This could mean giving childcare offices inside the organization so that guardians could deal with their youngsters in their mid-day break or between gatherings.

By working on the similarity of family and work, the generally speaking nurturing quality will probably be moved along.

Simultaneously, these organizations will turn out to be more alluring for profoundly qualified workers, which might give them a benefit in the battle for ability.

Cultivate homes

In particularly serious situations where guardians can't deal with their youngsters by any means because of substance addiction or different issues, safeguarding these kids by removing them from their homes and bringing them up in encouraging homes might be sensible.

In any case, it must be guaranteed that the nature of these encouraging homes is high and kids have adequate degrees of care so they can foster in a sound way.

Mental help

In the event that guardians experience the ill effects of mental issues, it could likewise be useful to give them mental help.

Not exclusively will this work on the general personal satisfaction of guardians, yet it might likewise further develop the nurturing quality for youngsters since assuming intellectually debilitated guardians seek help and legitimate treatment, they might have the option to care more for their kids.

Monetary appropriations

Guardians who experience the ill effects of outrageous degrees of destitution ought to likewise set monetary help for their youngsters up to give them instructive materials and different things important to allow these kids a fair opportunity for a decent future.

This could likewise come as training vouchers so that guardians can't spend the cash on liquor or medications all things being equal and it tends to be guaranteed that the cash is spent on things that really benefit youngsters from troublesome family conditions.

Programs against drug use

For guardians who are dependent on drugs, there ought to be sufficient detoxification revolving around so that guardians who will stop substance addiction track down help to accomplish this troublesome mission.

This isn't just valid for guardians, yet in addition for youngsters which are as of now dependent on substances.

In addition, there ought to likewise be programs that expect to forestall the underlying first utilization of medications, since this may likewise forestall possible future addictions.

Self-reflection

A certified self-reflection is essential to prevail in all pieces of life.

Everybody of us has imperfections and inadequacies, notwithstanding, realizing them is imperative.

Provided that you know your defects, you can begin to battle them in a legitimate way.

This is likewise valid for terrible nurturing.

Provided that you investigate yourself consistently and ask yourself what you can improve, can you work on the general nature of nurturing over the long run.

Self-advancement

Firmly connected with self-reflection is the subject of self-advancement.

Whenever you have recognized your inadequacies, attempting to further develop these deficiencies is vital to further develop your in general nurturing quality.

This ought to likewise incorporate conversing with different guardians and how they take care of explicit issues so you get a more extensive view on the particular point and can likewise incorporate valuable exhortation into your nurturing technique.

Upgrades in training

To battle the awful nurturing issue, it is vital to further develop the general instruction levels.

By working on generally speaking training, individuals might be better ready to recognize their own weaknesses and to deal with it to self-work on themselves and their nurturing style.

Support youngsters in your area

You shouldn't just attempt the best for your kids, yet additionally support different kids in your local area who appear to have difficult issues at home.

Assuming you distinguish these kids, attempt to help them.

This could intend to illuminate their school about their concerns or additionally to converse with their folks since many guardians may not actually know about numerous issues their youngsters could really need to manage.

End

Terrible nurturing is a critical issue in our general public these days.

Many guardians are just wrecked by their own concerns and neglect to treat and support their kids in a legitimate way.

Thus, it is urgent that establishments like schools or different offices go to lengths to help youngsters from troublesome family conditions.

Really at that time will it be feasible to further develop the in general nurturing quality over the long haul for some youngsters around the world.

Chapters 6

Family cause the destiny destroyer

Thinking back to our folks, grandparents, and incredible grandparents, we can frequently follow our actual elements, assets, and shortcomings through the family line. Similarly, we can notice character attributes and otherworldly impacts that range the ages. A Genuine legacy offers a solid underpinning of uprightness and loyalty, yet deeds like indignation, desire, and harshness set damaging examples that should be perceived and survived.

In the Scriptural record of Abraham's family, the wrongdoing of trickery turned into a fortification that impacted the existences of Abraham, Isaac, Jacob, and Jacob's children. (See Beginning 12:10-20, 20, 26:1-11, 27:1-40, 37:12-36.) Then again, the New Confirmation instances of Lois, Eunice, and Timothy exhibit the wealth of a legacy of confidence. (See II Timothy 1:5.)

At the point when we comprehend what our lives are meant for by our ancestors, we can answer fittingly to that impact. We ought to appreciate and praise the decency that has gone down through our families. Additionally, we ought to recognize the evildoings of our ancestors, atone of our own wrongdoings, and attempt to defeat the propensities toward explicit sins that we have acquired. While we are not considered answerable for the wrongdoings of our predecessors, we are powerless to their weak spots and ought to be aware of these tendencies.

Recognize Generational Evildoings

At the point when God gave the Ten Charges to the country of Israel, He incorporated this depiction of His personality and ways: ". . . I the Master thy God am an envious God, visiting the evildoing of the dads upon the youngsters unto the third and fourth era of them that disdain me; and having pity unto great many them that adoration me, and keep my edicts" (Departure 20:5-6). God rehashes this admonition about generational evildoings in Mass migration 34:6-7, Numbers 14:18, and Deuteronomy 5:9-10.

What we do matters to the future, since kids have a characteristic propensity to copy their folks. At the point when guardians accomplish something wrong, their youngsters are probably going to legitimize a similar activity. Truth be told, they frequently legitimize significantly more damaging perspectives and activities, going past what their folks considered passable.

The most distinctive illustration of this impact is found in Adam's transgression. "Wherefore, as by one man sin went into the world, and demise by wrongdoing; thus passing passed upon all men, for that all have trespassed" (Romans 5:12). Due to Adam's choice in the Nursery of Eden to ignore God's order, every individual on earth has acquired a nature of resistance to God.

An illustration of how our progenitors' activities can impact us for good is tracked down in the seventh section of Jews: ". . . Levi likewise, who receiveth tithes, paid tithes in Abraham. For he was at this point in the flanks of his dad, when Melchisedec met him" (Jews 7:9-10). Despite the fact that Levi was not brought into the world until numerous years after Abraham and Melchisedec met, he is credited with paying offerings since he was an actual piece of Abraham when Abraham paid the offerings.

This idea rests at the core of our acquired assets and shortcomings. Since we are an actual piece of our progenitors, we are profoundly impacted by their choices and the examples of their lives. We can see this impact obviously in Abraham's loved ones.

Gain From the Declaration of Abraham, Isaac, and Jacob

Abraham is known as the Companion of God and the "father of all them that accept." (See James 2:23 and Romans 4:11.) His honest reactions and acquiescence in the significant choices of his life satisfied God. Be that as it may, when Abraham went down to Egypt because of starvation, he embraced a misleading practice.

What's more, it happened, when he [Abraham] was approached go into Egypt, that he said unto Sarai [Sarah] his significant other, See now, I know that thou workmanship a fair lady to view: subsequently it will happen, when the Egyptians will see you, that they will say, This is his better half: and they will kill me, however they will save you alive. Say, I ask you, thou workmanship my sister: that it could be well with me for thy purpose; and my spirit will live on account of you (Beginning 12:11-13).

Abraham's trickery put Sarah in moral danger, and Pharaoh adequately reproached Abraham when the falsehood was found. Years after the fact, Abraham utilized this untruth again when he and Sarah went to Gerar. (See Beginning 20.) In the two circumstances, God moved to shield Sarah and others from the wrongdoing of infidelity, yet in the years to come the evildoing of trickiness assumed a critical part in the existence of Abraham's relatives.

Abraham and Sarah's child Isaac followed Abraham's model and lied about the character of his better half, Rebekah, when they went in Gerar: "And the men of the spot requested him from his significant other; and he said, She is my sister: for he dreaded to say, She is my significant other; in case, said he, the men of the spot ought to kill me for Rebekah; since she was reasonable to view" (Beginning 26:7). At the point when the Philistine lord, Abimelech, found Isaac's trickery, he reprimanded Isaac for presenting different men to the conceivable sin of infidelity. (See Beginning 26:9-10.)

In the future, the untruths were coordinated toward close relatives. Rebekah and her child Jacob plotted to delude Isaac into giving secondborn Jacob the firstborn gift that legitimately had a place with Esau. Exploiting Isaac's faltering visual perception, Jacob bamboozled his own dad: "And he came unto his dad, and said, My dad: and he said, Here am I; who crafts thou, my child? Furthermore, Jacob said unto his dad, ``I'm Esau thy firstborn; I have done proportionately as thou badest me: emerge, I supplicate you, sit and eat of my venison, that thy soul might favor me" (Beginning 27:18-19).

Many years after the fact, Jacob's children bamboozled him concerning the government assistance of his child, Joseph. The more seasoned siblings, envious of Joseph's approval with Jacob, sold Joseph as a slave: "And they took Joseph's jacket, and killed a youngster of the goats, and plunged the coat in the blood; and they sent the layer of many tones, and they carried it to their dad; and said, This have we found: know now whether it be thy child's jacket or no. Furthermore, he knew it, and said, It is my child's jacket: an abhorrent monster hath gobbled up him; Joseph is without uncertainty lease in pieces" (Beginning 37:31-33). Not until years after the fact did

Jacob find the reality of what had befallen Joseph. (See Beginning 45:26.)

In these models, we can perceive how the wrongdoing of misdirection was taken up by an endless flow of ages, extending and turning out to be more frantic as the years progressed.

Recognize the Transgressions of the Ancestors

Nehemiah, Jeremiah, Daniel, and others comprehended that God believed them should concur with Him about the evildoings of their folks and reason to not proceed with them. These godly men recognized the injustices of their dads when they admitted their transgressions:

In the days when Nehemiah attempted to remake the walls of Jerusalem, Ezra the cleric assembled individuals and read to them out of the Law of God. At the point when they understood how far they had wandered from God's precepts, they apologized: "And the seed of Israel isolated themselves from all outsiders, and stood and admitted their transgressions, and the wrongdoings of their dads" (Nehemiah 9:2).

At the point when Jeremiah understood that God's hand of judgment was upon the place where there is Judah, he recognized the injustices of their ancestors. He implored, "We recognize, O Ruler, our insidiousness, and the wrongdoing of our dads: for we have trespassed against you" (Jeremiah 14:20).

At the point when Daniel perceived by the Sacred writings that it was the ideal opportunity for Israel to be re-established in the land, he looked for the Ruler's pardoning through petition and request, with fasting. He supplicated, "O Master, as per all thy honesty, I entreat you, let thine outrage and thy fierceness be gotten some distance from thy city Jerusalem, thy blessed mountain: in light of the fact that for our transgressions, and for the evildoings of our dads, Jerusalem ,and thy individuals are turned into a rebuke to all that are about us" (Daniel 9:16).

Perceive Moral Obligation

As we recognize the wrongdoings of our ancestors, we should likewise acknowledge moral obligation regarding our transgressions. For instance, a child can't fault his dad for his

transgression, nor could a dad at any point fault his child. God will manage every individual on the benefits of his own decisions. "In those days they will say no more, The dads have eaten a sharp grape, and the youngsters' teeth are set tense. However, everyone will kick the bucket for his injustice: each man that eateth the acrid grape, his teeth will be set tense" (Jeremiah 31:29-30).

This reality carries explanation to God's alerts about visiting evildoing people in the future, which Jeremiah rehashes in the following part: "Thou showest lovingkindness unto thousands, and recompensest the wrongdoing of the dads into the chest of their youngsters after them: the Incomparable, the Powerful

God, the Master of hosts, is his name, extraordinary in counsel, and strong in work: for thine eyes are open upon every one of the methods of the children of men: to give each one as per his methodologies, and as per the product of his doings" (Jeremiah 32:18-19).

Generational wrongdoings keep the laws of the gather: we get what we really ask for, we harvest where we sow, we procure more than we sow, and we procure in an unexpected season in comparison to what we sow.

"Be not deluded; God isn't taunted: for at all a man soweth, that will he likewise procure. For he that soweth to his tissue will of the tissue harvest debasement; however, he that soweth to the Soul will of the Soul procure life never-ending" (Galatians 6:7-8).

Track down Opportunity in Jesus Christ

At the point when we become mindful of the transgressions of our ancestors, we ought to answer in the accompanying ways:

. Understanding our ancestors' transgressions gives us the knowledge to get some distance from those particular perspectives and activities. We should concentrate on the Sacred texts to figure out how we can respect God here. Frequently we might have to construct limits in our lives to assist with shielding us from the enticements that are normal in our experience (for instance, compulsions to tipsiness, tattle, burglary, or unethical behavior). As we put away exercises that are current enticements here, our inclination toward generational sin examples will reduce.

The ability to beat generational sins comes simply by Jesus Christ. The Messenger Paul energizes us, "Put ye on the Ruler Jesus Christ, and make no arrangement for the tissue, to satisfy the desires thereof" (Romans 13:14).

Jesus said: "Verily, verily, I say unto you, Whosoever committeth sin is the worker of wrongdoing. Also, the worker abideth not in the house until the end of time: but rather the Child abideth for eternity. Assuming the Child in this manner will make you free, ye will be very free" (John 8:34-36).

www.ingramcontent.com/pod-product-compliance
Lightning Source LLC
LaVergne TN
LVHW052101160826
845678LV00015B/3312

* 9 7 9 8 3 5 5 3 0 8 4 7 6 *